PLEASE DON'T SAY YOU LOVE ME

Seant'a Conyers

Publishing Services By: Pen Legacy®
Cover By: Christian Cuan
Formatting By: U Can Mark My Word Editorial Services
Editing Services By: Candice "Ordered Steps" Johnson

Library of Congress Cataloging – in- Publication Data has been applied for.

ISBN: 9781736411209

PRINTED IN THE UNITED STATES OF AMERICA.

DEDICATION

This book is dedicated to God. When I had nothing and no one in my life, God kept me.

Three years ago, a horrific tragedy almost caused me to lose my mind. Instead of checking on me, the very ones I trusted laughed and gossiped about my pain…but God kept me! On the days when I could barely pry myself from the bed simply to go to work and function, God was my strength. I'm nothing without Him.

Everything I've accomplished is by the grace of God. Thank You, Lord, for removing negativity from my life and replacing it with better, even when I didn't understand what You were doing. You've turned my pain into peace and birthed purpose from my pain.

If you are dealing with loneliness, depression, or a broken heart and don't know where to begin your healing process, I encourage you to read your Bible and turn to God. He will make your crooked path straight, just as He did for me.

All glory goes to You, God. Thank You for loving me!

PLEASE
DON'T SAY
YOU LOVE ME

INTRODUCTION

I'm a fiercely private person.

The thing about me is, I don't meddle in other people's business so they won't feel comfortable inserting themselves into mine. Life's more peaceful that way. Peace isn't a dream for me; it's a lifestyle.

I've dealt with so much strife in my life that peace is crucial. I don't care if it's family or friends; anyone threatening my peace is expendable. After surviving a seven-year abusive relationship, years of heartbreak, childhood trauma, toxic relationships, and navigating through a painful divorce, I have zero tolerance for strife.

Enduring extensive heartbreak has enabled me to handle life on my terms. I was once a very broken woman, determined to fix myself. However, two years ago, my life took a drastic turn, leaving me with little hope for recovery. Either I'd get help, or I wouldn't survive.

I've always been the woman who is there for everyone else, but when I was at my lowest, help ran dry. Admittedly, I've always kept adversity to myself, especially heartbreak and hurt. If anything bad was happening in my life, the only ones who knew about it were God and me. I mastered dealing with struggles on my own, so other people's feelings weren't sacrificed during my healing process. You know what they say: *Hurt people hurt people.* Since I've experienced so much pain, trust is difficult for me.

The few times I opened up and shared my heart with others, they either used it against me or gossiped about it with someone else. I have a powerful testimony that I've never considered sharing until a few years ago when I decided I'd had enough. It was time to make some drastic changes in my life, and those changes began with me.

As crazy as it sounds, I used to be ashamed of my pain. I was too embarrassed to testify, but I was compelled to share it in order to help someone else either overcome similar issues or prevent it from happening to them.

In the midst of my shame, God showed me why I

need to share my story.

When there's a calling on our life and God's waiting for our YES, when He's waiting for us to surrender our hearts to Him completely, the devil will work overtime to trap us in chaos because he has seen our future and what God is about to do for us. It's his job to distract us by keeping us so focused on our past and the current trauma we're in that we lose hope. But, again, that's his job; ours is not to listen to him.

My focus wasn't on what the devil wanted me to do – I kept it on God. In fact, I focused so much on Him that the devil manifested in my life as a mate. He was a man whom I believed embodied all the qualities I was looking for in a partner. However, I quickly learned never to look for the devil to show up rocking red horns and a cape. The devil comes as everything we've ever desired. He may not know our thoughts, but he hears our prayers.

…which allows him to use them against us.

In the beginning of my spiritual walk with God, He swiftly began removing people from my life. When God wants to bless us with better things and people in our lives, He'll give us instructions to release certain things. Instead of us following God's instructions meant for our good, we selfishly hang on to what He asks us to let go of out of fear of the unknown, including people. We would rather cling to toxic relationships, thinking we truly know the person we're with and negating the fact that they're poisonous to us. Instead of leaving the person alone, we settle, fearful that we can't replace the hollow relationship and will end up alone. When God intervenes, however, He always steps in with better for us than before.

A spiritual season is a reflection of change ordained by God. Just like natural seasons change each year, our lives must also change. God loves and wants the best for us. Not following His direction could potentially trap us in the season we're currently in until we do what He says.

"To everything there is a season, and a time to every purpose under Heaven: A time to be born, and a time to die, a time to plant, and a time to pluck up that which is planted; a time to kill, and a time to heal; a time to break down, and a time to build up; a time to weep, and a time to laugh; a time to mourn, and a time to dance. A time to cast away stones, and a time to gather stones together; a time to embrace, and a time to refrain from embracing; a time to get, and a time to lose; a time to keep, and a time to cast away; a time to rend, and a time to sew; a time to keep

silence, and a time to speak; a time to love, and a time to hate; a time of war, and a time of peace."
(Ecclesiastes 3:1-8)

There was a time in my life when I was desperate to be loved by a man, but God clearly told me a relationship wasn't what I needed during that season of my life. All I needed was His love, and He wanted me to be still. His way of getting me to be still was by removing certain people, places, and things from my life.

This point of my journey was HARD. The damage I suffered would've happened no matter what choices I made because God had already written it. He knew the obstacles I had to endure and what I needed to go through to write my story.

Blessed are the pure in heart, for they will see God. Having a pure heart means you are blameless, unstained from guilt, where your thoughts, desires, purpose, will, understanding, and character resides. To be pure in heart means being blameless in who we are.

Hiding our flaws and problems only makes matters worse. When we meet someone under false pretenses, sooner or later, our true heart will inevitably reveal itself. People who pretend to be someone other than themselves can only fake for so long; eventually, they slip back into their true character. That's why it's best just to be who God calls us to be.

CHAPTER ONE

LOVE

What is love?

That's one of the most asked questions every day, whether questioning ourselves or asking others. Much of our life is spent searching for the elusive emotion that can either prove to be life-changing…or fatal. Sometimes we fall in love several times, thinking the person we have fallen in love with is our future spouse. We spend years in toxic relationships, wondering where Mr. or Mrs. Right is, only to be devastated when they don't show up. No one wants to go through life alone. Everyone wants to meet their soulmate, right?

Sound familiar?

Is that you?

I know it describes me.

"Love is patient, love is kind. It does not envy, it does not boast, it is not proud. It does not dishonor others, it is not self-seeking, it is not easily angered, it keeps no record of wrongs."

1 Corinthians 13:4-5

When I read that scripture, I always try to remember when I was loved in such a manner.

Are you in the kind of marriage the above scripture describes? If so, hold on to your spouse, because these days, this agape kind of love is rare. I'm not saying it's impossible, because...

"All things are possible with God."

Matthew 19:26

What I am saying, however, is we invest more in material things than we do to maintain healthy relationships. Love is secondary to labels. Many people use the finer things they can get from their mate as a measuring stick for the love they'll give them. Let me give you an example:

When searching for a life partner, what the potential mate has to offer tops the requirement list—

even ahead of acknowledging their heart or character. What if we meet two different individuals we're interested in dating? Both potential mates have jobs and are around the same age. One works at McDonald's, making $10.00 an hour. The other works for a Fortune 500 company making six figures.

Which one would you choose?

In my past, I wouldn't have given the McDonald's employee a chance. In fact, for most of my life, I've dated drug dealers. Back then, I figured why not? They provided me with the luxurious things I wanted, and that's what mattered to me the most. I've always dated who was familiar to me. However, after several toxic relationships, I woke up and changed my standards, hoping to find a better man. I didn't care what he had to offer me; I just wanted him to have a pure heart, good character, and be kind beyond measure.

DON'T SAY YOU LOVE ME

"Please don't tell me you love me" is a phrase some of us have said to someone. When love is abused, it can do more damage than getting punched in the face. You ever hear people tell someone they barely know *I love you*? This proves how many

people don't know the true meaning of those three little words.

What is love?

First of all, love is unconditional. Let's define unconditional before diving into what love really is.

Unconditional means not subject to conditions, which in terms of relationships, translates to loving others in spite of their mistakes and flaws, which is not without its challenges. Mistakes and flaws provoke us into giving up on people; unconditional means loving people for who they are. Yes, there will be parts of that person we won't like, but love them anyway through the good, the bad, and the *worst*.

Unconditional love is challenging, especially when the ugly side of folk makes us fall out of love with them. Everyone has an ugly side to them. What happens when we meet it? Do conditions make us let go, or do we hang on as if we don't see it? The ultimate decision is also one of the most difficult parts of being in love.

See, we desire love but run from the hard work that tags along for the ride. That's why it's crucial to fall in love with a person's heart and not their material possessions. Love is a complex set of emotions, behaviors, and beliefs. It is affection, protection, warmth, and respect for the one holding your heart.

Last but not least, love is a feeling, but it needs to be seen and not just felt.

It's nearly impossible for selfish people to fall in love. Why? Because selfish people love themselves more than their mate. A selfish person will receive unconditional love before they receive without strings attached. However, they only give to get back. Especially their hearts. Unconditional love can't flow from selfishness. In fact, selfishness blocks it. An unselfish person cares more about the other person's happiness and will do anything to give them peace and happiness without expecting anything in return.

That's unconditional love.

Now, I'm not limiting love to marriage. There's love of family, friends, or relationships, too. And if it's misused, love hurts no matter where it comes from. For instance, consider children who are abused and neglected by their parents. Think of how that makes them feel. Or maybe the friend who says they love you but then turns around and gossips about you to the next person. This is the kind of love that hurts. When a person tells you that they love you, then breaks your trust and mistreats you, it's heartbreaking. Sometimes the hurt produces pain they never recover from.

I spent three years of my life in a relationship

19

where I was told that I was loved, but I didn't understand actions not matching the words. I don't understand it now either. I also spent thirty years being told *I love you* by people I called friends or considered family. I've come to realize I literally spent forty years trying to figure out what love is.

I didn't know I was equating pain with love. Please understand pain is NOT love. We may be used to it, like picking out what we're wearing for the day, but that doesn't make it right. It's not normal. Suffering isn't love.

Sometimes love hurts. If we've ever been in love, chances are we've hurt somebody. It's alright to admit our part in it. But someone intentionally hurting us may be an indication that the pain they cause is their version of love. We're all humans who sometimes do and say hurtful things to each other, but it's not love! Crying every day or being miserable because the one who claims to love us is hurting us is a sure sign that we are in a toxic relationship. We must recognize how we're being treated.

…or mistreated.

LIFE IS WHAT WE MAKE IT

Life's what we make it.

More often than not, we create our own strife by

remaining in friendships, relationships, or dealing with family who continuously hurt us because we love them. Now I'll agree that the Bible instructs us to love those who hurt and use us, including our enemies.

"But I tell you, love your enemies, bless those who curse you, do good to those who mistreat you and persecute you."

Matthew 5:44

Let me help somebody:

The scripture says to "do good" by your enemies and don't mistreat them. It doesn't say to stay in the relationship and continue being mistreated. You can leave a toxic friendship or relationship no matter if it's family, friends, or even dissolving a marriage, which is the most difficult relationship to end.

Marriage is a vow between you, God, and your spouse. I had a hard time filing for divorce because I felt so much anguish over my broken vows. Those vows meant everything to me, as well as what God says about marriage. So, it took me a little longer to make the decision to divorce because I worried about disappointing Him. But I had to do what was best for me in order to heal and live.

And living meant saving my soul from blindly

believing a man who claimed to love me.

THE POWER OF I LOVE YOU

Let's admit that when someone says *I love you*, we believe them, right? I know I do. Why wouldn't we?

I love you has power. Upon hearing it, we trust the person who said it, feeling comfort and security. Then those three little words tear down the walls past hurt and pain built, one brick at a time. And when the bricks come crashing down, we feel secure within ourselves, as well as the person we love. Feeling safe and secure is one of the best parts of love because that's when love becomes beautiful.

We all want to be loved by someone special in our lives. The truth is, we're all loved — just not always in the form of a significant other. The Bible indicates that everyone won't be married.

"But I wish everyone were single, just as I am. But God gives to some the gift of marriage, and to others the gift of singleness."

1 Corinthian 7:7

Unfortunately, this scripture isn't mentioned or taught in churches. The most commonly used messages regarding marriage revolve around women waiting for their husbands to find them. As such, we are taught to prepare, so when our potential husbands find us, we'll be ready to be a good wife.

The sad truth is, many women grow impatient and go in search of their husbands because society harps on women becoming wives. I never went looking for my husband; he found me. Marriage was never a desire of mine, but I knew it was the correct thing to do in God's eyes so that I would not fall into the sin of fornication. The problem with my situation was I believed I was following God's instructions when it came to my marriage.

My significant other, however, was not.

Most women desire to be married. Some of us are even told we *need* a husband. But if we read further in the Bible, we'll find out society got it wrong.

"So I say to those who are not married and to widows, it is better to stay unmarried, just as I am. But if they cannot control themselves, they should go ahead and marry. It is better to marry than to burn with lust."

1 Corinthians 7:8-9

The scripture goes on further to say:
"An unmarried man can spend his time doing the

Lord's work and thinking how to please him. But a married man has to think about his earthly responsibilities and how to please his wife. His interests are divided. In the same way, a woman who is no longer married or has never been married can be devoted to the Lord and holy in body and in spirit. But a married woman has to think about her earthly responsibilities and how to please her husband. I am saying this for your benefit, not to place restrictions on you. I want you to do whatever will help you serve the Lord best, with as few distractions as possible."

1 Corinthians 7:32-35

THE TESTIMONY

I've spent the last two years of my life in chaos.

Chaos I didn't see coming.

I've taught myself to watch for red flags in everything I do. Unfortunately, those flags failed to help me see the destruction headed my way.

Two years ago, I was left mentally, physically, emotionally, and financially bankrupt. The only thing I had left to hang on to that kept me from losing my mind was my spirituality. Thank God I have a personal relationship with Him. If it hadn't been for God, I'm not sure I would be here today to share my story.

See, I was abandoned and left with no explanation other than I was too much, which left me empty inside. Completely numb, I was too broken to even shed a tear. At first, all I was trying to do was understand why, but just like everything else in my life, the why always comes later.

Journal Talk with God After the Chaos

Dear God,

I know I shouldn't question You, but I often catch myself wondering why You picked me? What do You see in me that others don't? You created me. Five years ago, I gave my heart to You, so I know you see the kind of heart that I have. I try to remind myself daily that though Your heart is pure and kind, people still saw fit to crucify You.

I spend most days alone, crying my eyes out and looking for answers to so many questions. I'm sure even if You gave me the answer, it still wouldn't make sense to me. I know this life I live isn't for me to understand, and I don't.

I spend every day working a job I absolutely hate. I start my days wondering who's going to use or mistreat me. It's sad to live always wondering what new person will dislike me today for absolutely no reason. I give my all, Lord, and no matter what I do or say, it's never good enough. I was born into a family who hates me for simply being who You created me to be: a petite, powerful, light-skinned girl.

If only I could get people to understand that I didn't choose myself. You chose me and created me in Your image. I was born in purpose. The same purpose others try to use to destroy me.

Why, God?

Why does Your will make them angry with me? I didn't ask for Your grace or favor.

I know that You have work for me to do, and I want to do it well. You have purposed my pain, which I walked in until one year ago when it all came flooding back. Now I am questioning, "Why, God?"

Why would You reopen old wounds? Why let a man come into my life and disrupt it when I was focused on You? I've overcome so much pain in my past. Why? Why did You allow me to suffer yet again?

Now I'm left questioning my worth, asking myself what I did wrong. God, I'm broken yet again. What do You want me to do this time with my brokenness? I'm lost, confused, embarrassed, hopeless, and ashamed of my story once again. I just want to understand, even though it's not my own understanding I should be in search of.

I know I shouldn't question what You've allowed. I'm trying to remember Your promises, Lord. In spite of reading Your Word daily, fasting, and praying, I still wake up every single day lost with questions and no answers. I don't hear from You, and I don't feel Your presence.

What did I do to anger You, Lord? God, where are You?

Where did I go wrong? I'm on my knees crying and begging You to heal me from this pain. Why are You so distant, God? Why is it that when I need You the most, You're gone? I'm crying out for you to please help me, Lord!

Please help me!

Do you hear me, Lord?

What did I do? What do You want me to do?

God finally speaks: "Be still, My child, and know that I am your God." (Psalm 46:10)

This was the day my life changed. It was this day I realized I left God; He hadn't left me.

Does my prayer sound familiar?

I was weak, but I was STRONG. Those were the words I wrote to God as my life fell apart again.

Why, God? Why?

Have you ever asked God why?

The hardest thing in life is finding yourself in a storm.

My biggest challenge was pulling myself out of a dark place. From that moment on, God showed me what strength truly is. I was looking for strength and God told me: "I AM STRENGTH."

STRENGTH

What is strength? How do you know if you have it?

The dictionary defines strength as the quality or state of being physically strong. Strength is more than physical. It's being mentally, emotionally, and spiritually strong.

Sometimes gaining physical strength is easy. Lifting weights or daily workouts strengthen our bodies, but we can still be left spiritually, emotionally, and mentally weak.

Strength is overcoming bad habits. Strength is overcoming addictions. Strength is forgiving yourself for settling for less than what you deserve. Strength is believing in yourself when others do not. Strength is learning to love yourself when others do not. Strength is persevering when you feel like giving up! Strength is knowing you are enough when others say you're nothing. Strength is overcoming past hurts and pains.

Strength is knowing who you are and not who others say you are.

This is what strength means and so much more — like receiving salvation and reconciling your soul to God, or discovering your truth. To discover our strength, we first need to learn to live our truth. It takes massive strength to be honest with ourselves and transparent with others to overcome the judgment that accompanies living in our truth.

A personal relationship with God gives us righteousness and indescribable strength. Strength is learning to encourage oneself. Others won't always be around to encourage and keep us uplifted. Once we learn to encourage ourselves, strength will follow. Strength provides us with the newness that our old lives couldn't live up to. We must gain the strength to create new lives for ourselves.

Additionally, growth requires massive strength. In order to grow in all areas of our lives, we must have the strength to release people, places, and things that are not of God and not good for us. When we can accomplish all of these things, that's strength. Most people have a hard time letting go. Strength gives us the opportunity to share our testimony with others. The moment we can be transparent in front of others is the moment we gain strength. Then we'll be strong enough to shake the shame people try to make us feel about our past. They only have the power to negate what we've overcome if we give them the power to do it.

Healing is the most important tool to gain strength. To heal, we must be willing to lay all the good, the bad, and ugliness in our life without feeling ashamed. Quite often, healing follows the testimony. Discussing our trauma relieves our pain and propels us to heal. Years of suffering takes mighty strength to overcome, but it's not impossible.

"Be strong and courageous. Do not fear or be in dread of them, for it is the Lord your God who goes with you. He will not leave you or forsake you."

Deuteronomy 31:6

Strength is having: **S** – Salvation
T – Truth
R – Righteousness
E – Encouragement
N – Newness
G – Growth
T – Testimony
H – Healing

God said, "My grace is sufficient for you, for My power is made perfect in weakness." Therefore, I will boast even more gladly about my weaknesses, so that Christ's power may rest on me. That is why, for Christ's sake, I delight in weaknesses, in insults, in hardships, in persecutions, in difficulties. For when I am weak, then

2 Corinthians 12:9-10

I have made a fool of myself, but you drove me to it. I ought to have been commended by you, for I am not in the least inferior to the "super-apostles," even though I am nothing."

2 Corinthians 12:11

CHAPTER TWO

THE MEET-N-GREET

January 2015 began a new life for me.

I had just ended a three-year toxic relationship and was content with not dating. I was good being single; my life was completely peaceful.

Early one July afternoon, a friend and I planned to meet at a restaurant for brunch. She called about an hour before it was time for us to meet, stating she had to cancel due to a family emergency. I was disappointed, but I understood. It was such a nice, warm day with the sun shining brightly and a cool breeze. Since my plans were canceled, I decided to take a stroll through the park.

This was around eleven o'clock in the morning, so I figured the park wouldn't be too packed. I threw my tennis shoes on, jumped in my car, and drove to Jackson Morrow Park, eager for my walk. When I arrived at the park, it was empty just as I expected, except for a few people on the walking trail. Perfect! I hopped out of my car, stretched, and headed out on the trail.

As I jogged, I realized my tennis shoes were untied. When I stopped running and bent over to tie them, I was startled by a large pair of tennis shoes standing directly in front of me, and I quickly bolted up.

"Excuse you?" I fussed at the dark, handsome, clean-cut man before me. "Why are you just standing there? You scared me half to death!"

I was just fussing at this man, who kept calm without a word, but his dazzling smile said everything I needed to hear.

"So, are you just going to stand there and say nothing?" I prodded.

"I apologize for scaring you," his deep voice uttered. "I was admiring your beauty. I noticed you when you got out of your car, but before I could make it over to introduce myself, you were already jogging down the trail. Since you stopped running, I figured this was the perfect time. I really do apologize if I startled you."

34

While he spoke, I stared at this man, thinking to myself how fine he was and not paying attention to a word he said. I finally quit daydreaming and snapped to reality.

When he finally stopped talking, the only thing I could think to say was, "Why are you bothering me?"

The shock on his face said that wasn't what he expected to hear. Shoot, I surprised myself because I really wasn't trying to say that. I just blurted out what was on my mind.

"Guess that surprised you, didn't it?" I asked, staring into his gorgeous eyes without flinching.

"Yes," he answered.

"Well, I really am wondering why you're bothering me?" I repeated, still waiting on an answer.

He apologized for approaching me, but it wasn't enough to pacify me.

Why was I being so mean to a man who was so fine?

After coming out of such a toxic relationship, I was comfortable being single and not ready to dive into another one. I'd gotten my relationship with God together, and I was okay if He never sent me a husband, because I didn't want to get married. If it happened, I would be fine with it, but it wasn't a requirement for my happiness.

During my quiet time with God, I spent a lot of time in His Word. And His Word confirmed that not every man or woman would marry.

"For now, stay put. Be content in the situation where God has placed you. If you're married don't seek to be single. If you're single don't seek to be married. Live God's way, one day at a time and he will show you what to do."

1 Corinthians 7:3-11

According to scripture, I was on the right path. I wasn't worried about meeting a man and hoping he was my husband. My focus was strictly on God. That's why the fine man triggered me as opposed to turning me on.

As much as I would love to say the stranger walked away from me after I was so rude to him, he didn't. Instead, he laughed at me, which ticked me off. I wanted to jog off and leave him standing there alone. I'm not sure why I didn't.

"Excuse me, sir. What's so funny?"

Through a flurry of chuckles, he finally managed to answer, "*You.* I'm laughing at you, beautiful lady."

By this time, I was fuming. "Why am I so funny?"

"Your demeanor." He stifled another round of

laughs after spying the scowl on my face. "The way you're coming off as this rude young woman. It's not who you are."

Wow.

That was unexpected.

I stared at him as he continued laughing at me, wondering if I should punch him in the face or join in the laughter. I couldn't help myself; joy won.

"You know what? You're right," I said and burst into a fit of giggles.

Since he hadn't stopped, we ended up laughing until we almost cried.

"What's your name?" I asked once we settled down.

"Kevin," he responded with a gargantuan smile. "It's nice to meet you."

Kevin asked if I ventured to the park often and was shocked to find I had never been there.

"Well, I'm glad you decided to come today," he told me, as well as the fact that he went to the park every day to jog around the trail.

As Kevin spoke, I didn't tell him, but I didn't care what he had to say, even though I wanted to. In fact, while he was talking, I tied my shoes. Once he was done talking, I politely told him it was a pleasure to meet him, but I needed to finish my run so I could get home. He asked if he could join me, and of course, I wanted to deny him because I wasn't there to meet a man. But not wanting to be rude, I agreed to let him join me.

Instead of jogging, we decided to walk briskly. Kevin did most of the talking, oblivious that I really didn't want to be bothered. As we walked, he asked tons of questions like how old I was. At the time, I was forty-three, but he lied and said I couldn't be older than twenty-five. I blushed, but I still wasn't buying his bull. However, the more he spoke, the more curious I was about him — so curious that I got around to asking my own questions.

Kevin was thirty-nine and from the south. He explained how he was from Sikeston, Missouri. Sick of being surrounded by death and danger, and needing a change of scenery, he had transferred jobs. After he had divulged a few more facts about himself, I kept mine short and sweet.

I shared with him that I was a single mother with two boys, worked a full-time job (which I didn't divulge for safety purposes), and liked to write in my free time.

"That's it? That's all you're going to tell me about yourself?" he asked.

"Yep," I confirmed. "We've known each other less

than fifteen minutes. How do I know you're not a serial killer?"

Kevin laughed, then extended me an invitation to get to know him better over lunch.

I abruptly stopped walking, looking at him like he was crazy. "I don't know about that," I nervously answered.

Kevin flashed that glorious smile again, easing my skepticism. "It's going to be at a busy public place. Completely safe. I promise."

We stood in silence for a bit as I contemplated a thousand ways to reject his offer, but none of them seemed to be a fit. It was hot outside and awkward with Kevin staring in my face like he would be devastated if I declined his invitation. So, I accepted it on the condition we would only be going out once.

The grin Kevin had couldn't be purchased. He invited me to the Sycamore Grill downtown, and we set a date for the next day at noon. I don't know why, but on top of everything else, I let him walk me to my car.

So much for alone time.

Just as I started to say goodbye and get in the car, Kevin had another question for me.

"Wait a minute. I didn't get your number. How will I contact you if I can't make it, or something happens and I need to reschedule?"

Dang it, I hadn't given him the number on purpose so I could ditch him, and he couldn't track me down. I was busted and didn't have a choice. So, I gave up the digits.

And we solidified our date with a smile.

CHAPTER THREE

THE FIRST DATE

It was around nine o'clock on a Saturday morning. I got up, headed straight to the bathroom to freshen up, grabbed my Bible, read my daily devotion, and then said my morning prayers.

After I finished praying, I opened my front door to check the temperature outdoors. Despite the blazing sun, there was a nice summer breeze. It was bright and beautiful — everything I loved about summer. As I stood in the doorway, I decided to sit on the front porch for a while. As I enjoyed the steamy day, it hit me: I had a date.

I immediately grasped for reasons to call and cancel, but nothing sounded sincere enough for Kevin to believe me. He was so adamant about me getting to know him, even though I wasn't feeling him at all. It was nothing against him; I just wasn't interested in him or anyone. Life was going too good for me, and I was content with how things were. The longer I sat on the porch thinking, the more I realized what I needed to do was pray.

Dear Heavenly Father, I come to You asking for Your guidance. I need direction. I met a man yesterday while I was out jogging, and I need Your discernment and wisdom. Lord, if this man is not my husband, please remove him from my life. Lord, I do not want to waste more of my time pouring energy into toxic, meaningless relationships. Lord, I thank You for my answered prayers. In Jesus' name, I pray, Amen.

Praying makes me feel so much better. I ask God for direction, and He never fails to give it to me.

After praying, I zipped inside the house and got ready for my first date in years. As I dressed with gospel music blaring through Pandora, I was overcome with excitement. While making myself beautiful, I worshipped, cried, and praised God for being so amazing.

My bedroom was a complete mess, and I changed outfits at least five times, bugging my boys to tell me which one looked best before finally settling on jeans, heels, and a nice blouse. I checked the mirror a final time to make sure I looked okay before leaving.

After getting all dolled up for a man I didn't even want, I peered at my reflection and burst into laughter.

"Girl you're a mess," I giggled, then grabbed my keys and told my boys I was heading out.

After pulling up to the packed restaurant, a thousand reservations settled on my shoulders as I observed the crowded line of people waiting outside to get in. My nerves were up. The last thing I wanted to do was go through with this date, so I wasted time in the car until Kevin came up and knocked on the window.

"Hello, beautiful. I didn't startle you, did I?" he asked.

"I was just freshening up before I got out," I said as casually as I could. "It looks packed."

"Don't worry about the crowd," he assured me. "It's always this busy. Lucky for us, I made reservations."

At least he had planned ahead.

As we strolled up to the door, I found myself hoping I wouldn't run into anyone I knew. I wasn't in the mood to explain who Kevin was, how we met, or that we were on a date. By the grace of God, my prayers were answered. Now I just needed to get through this date.

It was obvious the restaurant was a place Kevin frequented. So many people greeted him and shook his hand while making small talk, but I was unimpressed.

"What are you shaking your head about?" I asked after delivering the news that this would be our only date before it got started.

"You haven't even given yourself a chance to get to know me, and you're already cutting me out of your life," Kevin chuckled.

"I told you I only agreed to go out with you because you were so adamant. Seriously, I felt forced."

He laughed so hard that he nearly doubled over. "I didn't force you to go out with me. I asked, and you agreed."

I rolled my eyes. "Yeah, whatever."

Just as I was about to let Kevin have it, the hostess called his name for us to head to our table. As we made our way through the restaurant, he was greeted by more acquaintances, stopping by their tables to have quick small talk. This was going to be a long afternoon.

We kept walking until we got to our table in the very back of the restaurant. We were in a private room with ten tables and five other people seated at them.

"Why are we in this private room?" I asked as Kevin pulled my chair out, and I took a seat.

"I requested that we be back here where it's quiet so we can talk without any interruptions."

"Interruptions?" My brows rose. "Who would be interrupting us?"

Ignoring my question, Kevin eased on in his chair with a smile. "Do you drink wine or alcohol?"

"Absolutely not," I declared with attitude.

After a bit of verbal ping pong about my aversion to liquor and what I wanted to drink, Kevin excused himself from the table and went to the bar to order our drinks.

"Who is this guy?" I wondered aloud while eyeing him at the bar. "What the heck have I gotten myself into?"

He talked to the bartender with ease and engaged everyone around him in light conversation. The way everyone treated him, it was almost as if Kevin was a celebrity. I may not have been interested in going on this date at first, but now, I wanted to know what he was all about. When he arrived back at our table with the drinks, I had questions.

"You look like something's on your mind," Kevin observed.

Sliding my glass back and forth in front of me, I decided to let him know what I was thinking.

"I want to know who you are. Tell me more about you."

"Oh, so now you're interested in me?"

"Of course," I reiterated with a grin. "It's like you're a celebrity or something. How do you know all these people?"

"I'm a licensed insurance representative," he explained in his deep tenor. "Those are my clients you saw me speaking to. When I moved here, the company gave me my own building next door to Sycamore Grill."

"Now it makes sense," I said with a nod.

Kevin grinned and continued with his story. "Since I was new to town and didn't know anybody, instead of sitting in my office all day waiting for clients to walk in, I came over here and networked at the bar until I built my clientele."

"So, how many clients do you have now?" I asked as I took a sip of my drink.

The light in Kevin's eyes said he was excited to have my sincere attention. It was about time.

"I went from zero clients to over a thousand in three months. I get so many customer referrals it's out of control, but I love it."

Kevin's ambition and drive impressed me; I was inspired by his story. As I gulped down the rest of my drink, I was amazed at how invested I was in this date that I didn't want to go on at first.

"Hey, you never told me your last name," I said, almost not recognizing my own flirty voice.

"Douglas. Kevin Douglas. Back home, I go by KD."

"I see. Do you have any children?"

Kevin nodded, his face beaming with pride. "One. A five-year-old daughter named Chanel. I love her so much."

Somehow, even in the crowded restaurant, it felt as if only the two of us were there. We exchanged details about ourselves, and I listened intently as Kevin shared that he had a sister and half-brother, was born in St. Louis but raised in Sikeston, Missouri, and both his parents were living.

"Our family is close," Kevin said. "I talk to my sister and mother every day. I've never been married, but I was in a ten-year relationship with Chanel's mother."

"So what happened?" I asked.

"We grew apart from each other and decided to go our separate ways."

"I get it." I replied while nodding. "Sometimes breakups are inevitable."

"Exactly," Kevin agreed.

Every other weekend, Kevin and Chanel's mother met in Kentucky, and he brought his daughter back to Indiana so they could spend time together. He also got her during the summer and on holidays.

The more we talked, the more comfortable I became with him. Kevin was so endearing. I realized he wasn't some creep just hitting on me. He was gentle and kind — the kind of man I could be with. But I still wasn't ready for a relationship. At least we could be friends. He was so easy to talk to, and I wasn't offended when he wanted to know more about me. However, I wasn't going to give up too much information.

"I'm glad I decided to go to lunch with you," I said, changing the subject. "You're a really nice guy. I enjoy your company."

"I'm happy to hear that," he said. "I enjoy being here with you, too."

After chatting a while, we finally ordered steaks and potatoes. Then we ate, laughed, talked, and enjoyed each other's company for about an hour.

After my initial reservations going into this, I felt silly. Being around Kevin felt wonderful.

"This has been fun, but I have to be back at work before two o'clock because I have an appointment with a new client," he said, regret filling his eyes.

"No worries," I acknowledged. "I've had a good time."

"Me, too."

We finished eating, and Kevin walked me out to my car. Like a gentleman, he opened the door for me and closed it once I settled inside.

"Seeing that we both had such a great time, would you like to meet up again?"

As much as I enjoyed our time together, I wasn't eager to rush into anything.

"Can I have time to think about it?"

"No pressure," he said, still upbeat.

I could tell he was a bit disappointed, though.

"May I call or text you?"

"Now that, I don't mind," I confirmed with a smile.

We agreed to begin there, and maybe in a few weeks meet back up if I felt comfortable. Then we said our goodbyes and went on about our day.

CHAPTER FOUR

AS THE TIME GOES BY

As the months flew by, Kevin and I got to know each other very well. He texted early mornings, late nights, and random times throughout the day. We met once or twice a month for lunch, which kept enough distance between us to keep from labeling what we had a relationship. That was fine with me because I wasn't interested in being anyone's girlfriend. I had become extremely comfortable being alone. My relationship with God was all I needed.

Whenever a man came into my life, I prayed and asked God to remove him if he wasn't my husband because I didn't want or need any distractions. My relationship with God was my priority, and I didn't want anything or anyone getting in my way of that.

After a few months, our conversations grew longer and more personal. Kevin revealed more information about himself without me asking, which caught me off guard. I never had to ask him questions; he volunteered what I wanted to know without me having to pull it out of him. I never second-guessed what he shared with me since marriage was the furthest thing from my mind. I was just letting a man be a man. It was his job to pursue me, and that's what I was letting him do.

Now don't get me wrong; Kevin was nothing like the other men I dated in the past. He was genuinely nice, loving, kind, educated, respectful, and had a great job. He never tried to have sex with me or even asked to sleep over at my house. However, I should've known the visage was too good to be true. I prayed every day, asking God for red flags and warning signs. I won't say He didn't give me any, but if He did, I wasn't paying attention.

Kevin was different. So much so, I wouldn't admit he was the man of my dreams to him because I wasn't looking for a relationship. That's probably why I got caught up in another toxic one. I will say this relationship was the worst I have ever dealt with because it ruined my life. I lost everything and was forced to rebuild my life, which was the hardest thing

I've ever done in my forty-four years of living.

It was the lowest I've ever been.

Kevin showered me with attention and time, constantly taking me out on dates. Everything about us felt like I was making the right decisions, and I truly believed I'd been chosen by the right man.

Why do I say I was chosen by the right man? Because in my opinion, a woman shouldn't hunt for a husband, which Biblically is the man's responsibility.

"He who finds a wife finds a good thing and obtain favor from the Lord."

Proverbs 18:22

The keyword in that scripture is **He**. The truth of the matter is, I picked every one of my former mates without God's help. I didn't want to make the same mistake again, but guess what?

Life happens.

Two years later, we were engaged.

He had proven himself to me and was the complete opposite of my mates from past relationships. We invested time in getting to know each other, and I believed I knew everything about him. Not for one moment did I feel like he was lying to me about anything or like there was more I needed to know about him. He had been incredibly open and transparent about his life with me.

...at least that's what I thought.

Even when I met Kevin's family, I didn't see any hidden agendas or felt uncertainty. The love his family had for him shined through, and it gave me all the feels. Even my friends and loved ones believed he was a great guy. I felt so blessed that I didn't discern the disaster headed my way. I guess the phrase "love makes you blind" is true. I was too blind to see the bad because for once in my life, I felt loved.

CHAPTER FIVE

THE MARRIAGE

Dear God,

Today's an exciting day full of love, laughter, and fun. Why? Because it's my wedding day! The day I've dreamt of for forty-two years. Finally, a great man found me and made me his good thing. A man who correctly pursued and courted me. An educated man who is a great father, respectful, has a good job, and most importantly, loves my children as his own, as well as You, Lord.

God, now I understand when people say the devil doesn't dress in a red cape and horns; he comes as everything we desire. After You healed me from brokenness and bad relationships, I'm finally ready for and deserve a good man. God, I have You in my life, guiding me and leading me along the way, and I'm thankful.

There's no way I can venture back down the path You delivered me from, God. I asked you every day when this man came into my life if he was my husband and prayed for You to remove him if he wasn't. I even mentioned that this was my prayer to him, and You know what he told me?

"You can keep praying for God to remove me, but I'm not going anywhere."

Now there we were, about to get married!

Lord, I don't want anything extravagant for my wedding — just an intimate, elegant ceremony with close family and friends. His favorite color is blue, and one of mine is silver. So, that's what we're going with. It's such a wonderful day, too! Surrounded by family and friends to celebrate our love in the simplest way. What more could I ask for?

Truthfully, I wanted a destination wedding, but since Kevin wanted to invite all his family, I gave him what he asked for. God, if I would've known that a year from today he would betray me nearly past the point of recovery, I wouldn't go through with it. Had I known I would be put in a position to lose all hope, there's no way I would've put myself through it.

But, one year after we married, my husband was

gone.

Apparently, me and my life were too much for Kevin to handle. At least that was the lame excuse he gave me. Marriage was too big of a responsibility for him, so he backed out after promising me forever. I was destroyed.

Why, God?

Why would You allow me to end up hurt again? I was content with my life the way it was before Kevin walked into it. I was okay with being single. I patiently waited for You to send me my husband, and in my heart, I knew it was him. I thought I was following Your direction, God. Where did I go wrong yet again? I'm tired of making the same mistakes and getting the same results.

Why, God? Where are You? Do You hear me, Lord? I thought this marriage was Your will? I cried out to You until I heard Your soft reply:

"Wait on Me next time, My child. If one gives an answer before he hears, it is his folly and shame."
Proverbs 18:13

Lord, all this time, I've blamed You, when I should have just stayed in Your will instead of my own.

CHAPTER SIX

Journal Talk with God After the Chaos

Dear God,

I should've known this day was going to end in disaster.

It was a stunning Sunday morning — Father's Day. My family and I got up and prepared for church, just like any other regular Sunday.

This particular Sunday church was special because with tears running down his face, my youngest son testified in front of the congregation how happy he was to have a father figure in his life. He was so happy my husband had found me; it was a touching testimony.

That day opened my eyes to a reality that I didn't realize. I didn't know how damaged my boys were because of their biological father's absence in their lives. All I ever tried to do was be a good mother. I knew I couldn't raise two boys to be men without the help of a man, which is why I did my best to include male mentors in their lives and kept them active in sports.

God, I don't know why you gave me two boys to raise out of wedlock. When they were conceived, I never imagined I would be left to raise them on my own. Of course, I'm the one who fell into sexual sin, but I still question why I've had to do this by myself.

That day, my family and I had a good time at church. After service, we planned a family barbecue, which I desperately looked forward to because my husband and I had an argument that had yet to be resolved. He said some hurtful things to me, God, and I was confused. While the kids were in the house, I sat outside with my husband to see if we could talk through and resolve our issues.

It seemed like as soon as I walked out on the back porch to join him, he was instantly irritated by my presence. That was when I realized communication would be the demise of our marriage. God, I just wanted to know what I did that was so wrong? Why had my marriage of one year taken a turn for the worse?

THE CHAOS

Honestly, I wish I could explain what happened to my marriage, but I can't because I really don't know. As crazy it sounds, I can't articulate the facts because not even I'm privy to them.

You may think to yourself, *something* destroyed their marriage, and you would be right. There's no way I can disagree. The thing is, I didn't know the person I married well enough. In chapter two, I mentioned that we spent a lot of time together, which we did. But spending time together doesn't equate to getting to know the person you're spending time with. People pretend well. Although I don't know what destroyed my marriage, I can describe what I went through and how it affected every facet of my life.

In all my years, I never believed I needed to perform an extensive background check on the men I was involved with. I've always thought that once a person reaches a certain age, they don't lie anymore. We're all adults, so we should be able to handle the truth, right?

Let me tell you — and this goes for men, too:

When entering into relationships, go beyond a criminal background check. If they claim to have graduated from high school or college, ask to see their diploma or degree. When meeting their family, pay close attention to what their loved ones say about them. If they say they have children, check to make sure they don't have more than they claim. People are out here in these streets creating imaginary lives, pretending to be someone they're not.

BE CAREFUL.

Remember, it only took thirty days for my life to take a drastic turn. Somehow, everything I'd overcome in my past circled back around, and I wasn't sure how I got back to the place where I was disrespected, talked about, and feeling ashamed with no one to lean on except God and myself. I returned to my dark place, with no hopes of getting out this time. It was the lowest I'd ever been in my entire life.

Father's Day weekend, my husband and I got into a horrible argument, and he left me. Little did I know when I watched him disappear out the door, it would be forever. I wouldn't want any woman in the world to experience the pain of her husband inexplicably walking out after only a year. No one should be subjected to the man who stood at the altar before God, claiming to love you until death do you part, vanishing without reason. My heart was ripped from my chest and torn in half; he stepped on it as he walked out the door.

Two weeks after Kevin was gone, I was still trying desperately to hang on to my marriage. I was afraid of disappointing God or that He'd be angry with me for my failed marriage. Every day I woke up asking Him for the strength to carry on as I tried not to slip into depression. This pain was different than before. This wasn't a boyfriend; Kevin was my husband. How could he leave that way? No explanation. Nothing. It's a question for which I'll never have the answer.

Amid the turmoil, I still had to work every day. I had a household to maintain and kids to care for. As a single mother again, there wasn't sufficient time to mourn my dead relationship. At first, I blamed myself, wondering where I went wrong. I had lots of questions, but no answers.

Work hours were spent struggling to keep myself together, some better than others. I was on the verge of having a nervous breakdown, but going on sick leave wasn't an option. In fact, going on leave would make things worse because I'd be sitting at home crying all day. Although every day was a struggle, I did it — by the grace of God. I was battered, broken down, and weak on the inside, but anyone who laid eyes on me only saw my strength. I never could've made it on my own; I owed everything to God.

Two weeks after Kevin abandoned me, I was at work when one of the machines on my line broke down. As the team lead, I was required to fix what was broken, and if I couldn't, I was supposed to write up a ticket to get a skilled tradesperson to help get the machine back up and running. After everything I had been through, the last thing I expected was to get my hand stuck in a hydraulic press welder for **five minutes**. All I could do was scream; it felt like I was near death. The tradesman helping me work on the machine commanded me to stop screaming and calm down, which helped me gain my composure. I began praying and asked God to save my hand. If you know anything about a hydraulic press, then you know I'm blessed that my hand wasn't amputated.

Due to the gruesome injury, I couldn't use my right hand, the dominant one, for months. Unfortunately, I suffered severe nerve damage beyond repair and probably wouldn't regain feeling in my hand again, according to my doctor. But if I did, it could take months or maybe even years. I had to learn how to write with my left hand, amongst other things, and endured months of physical therapy to regain strength back into my hand so I could use it again.

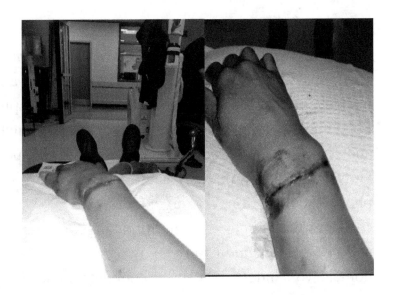

Within two weeks, I lost my husband and almost had my hand cut off. How much more could I take? Everything that could go wrong went wrong. *Why me?* Maybe God was punishing me for getting divorced. There were so many explanations for what I was going through, but I had zero answers once again.

God was silent.

I'm a strong woman, never one to throw pity parties because the last thing I want is to have folk feeling sorry for me. All I wanted was to be surrounded by love, but no one was there to extend it to me. I cried out to God every single day, not knowing what else to do. But I soldiered on.

There I was, heartbroken, injured, and still trying to help at work even with only one working hand. I was tired. Tired of being strong for my children and myself. Tired of my plans being thrown into a tailspin. I had book tours, photos, and video shoots scheduled, and it looked as if none of it was going to happen. However, a week after my hand injury, I received a phone call that I'll never forget.

It was a Thursday evening following my accident, and my children and I were enjoying time together at home. My oldest son was cooking dinner; my youngest was dancing to music. I received a call from my landlord of six years ordering me out of the house because of something Kevin had done. I tried explaining to him that he no longer resided in the home, but he wasn't trying to hear anything that I had to say even though I heard him out. Once he finished, I assured him we would vacate the house before the next month's rent was due.

In thirty days, my entire life changed faster than I could comprehend. Has something drastic ever shocked you so bad that you didn't even respond to it? That was me. I couldn't cry and didn't even get upset. After hanging up the phone, I simply strolled back into the kitchen and told the boys that we would be starting the process of moving out of our house the next day. Then we all carried on like we hadn't received any bad news.

The next morning, my youngest son and I were at the house while my oldest son went to work. After he left to go in, I went and rented the biggest moving truck I could find to move our three-bedroom, two-bath home. We moved the entire house by ourselves, except the couch because it was too heavy. That piece could wait to be moved until my oldest son finished his shift.

Unable to find another place on such short notice, we put our belongings in a storage unit across town. We had no idea where to go, so I asked my mother if it was okay for the boys to stay with her until I figured out where we were going to live, which made me feel like a complete failure. I had promised my boys that we would never be homeless again. Fourteen years later, we didn't have a place to call home.

I was determined to keep the promise that I had made to my children and refused to take them back to the homeless shelter we lived in when my youngest was eight months old. We stayed there for four months, and when we moved out of the shelter on his first birthday, I vowed we would never be in that position again.

Kevin never called to check on us or see if I needed

anything. I had no idea of his whereabouts, and he had no idea I moved out of the house. Not that he cared, but I couldn't worry about that. I had to get my life back together, even if it meant moving with no direction. All I knew was I had a lot on my plate, more than I could bear, and I needed God more than I ever needed Him before.

CHAPTER SEVEN

THE LIES

Have you ever been lied to? How did it make you feel? Do you ever wonder what causes people to lie to you? I say lies come from *selfishness*.

We know that lies cause hurt, pain, and mental damage. So why do people do it? These are questions we all think about when a person we love lies to us. The Bible says there are seven things that God hates:

"Seven that are abomination to Him: haughty eyes, a lying tongue, and hands that shed innocent blood, a heart that devises wicked plans, feet that make haste to run to evil, a false witness who breathe out

lies, and one who sows discord among brothers."
                                        Proverbs 6:16-19

Kevin was the man of my dreams. I loved absolutely everything about him — his smile, the way he walked, the way he talked, the way he carried himself. He was perfect in my eyes and could do no wrong. The thing is, liars don't come with tags indicating they're dishonest, like washing instructions attached to shirts. There's no certain look to sound the alarm so we'll know, but wouldn't it be nice if there was? It sure would save us a lot of time, but unfortunately, only time snitches on liars.

We've all dealt with liars more than once or twice in our lifetime. Now I can't speak for everyone else when it comes to being lied to, but I can certainly speak from my own experiences with manipulation and deceit.

Lies breed mental complications. They not only break trust; they cause issues in general. I wish I could answer why people lie, knowing their dishonesty could dismantle someone's well-being, or worse — ruin their life. I may not have the answers, but I know what deception does to a woman and how to persevere through it and rise to become the resilient queens we are after the pain.

My failed marriage isn't what hurt me. It was the lies behind it that broke my heart. See, I'm a very understanding person. Because I've been judged all my life, I try not to judge others. I know how it feels when people judge us before taking the time to get to know us. That's what led to me being the vulnerable, sometimes naïve woman I am. I tend to trust words instead of actions, which doesn't always end well. When we depend solely on the words of people we trust, we have to make adjustments or run the risk of hurting ourselves. Because once a liar learns you blindly trust them based on what they say, they'll use their words to manipulate you.

I'll never understand how liars can hurt or damage others, then behave as if they've done nothing wrong. God didn't design us to understand it, so stop trying. The only thing we can do is learn to watch people's actions more instead of relying on what they say.

Maya Angelou said it best: "When someone shows you who they are, believe them the first time."

In my situation, I didn't spot the hidden agendas through the love and respect I was being shown on the surface. I suppose love truly is blind. The ones we love consistently show us who they really are. It's up to us to receive the red flags and warning signs.

Most of us ignore the signs, then blame the liar for

what they've done to us. STOP. Now. Seriously, we must take responsibility for allowing some of the things that happen to us, even though we don't deserve it. We're in total control of how we allow people to treat us, and although we can't stop someone from mistreating us, we can control the way we respond.

One of the prayers I often hear quoted but don't believe many fully understand is:

"God, grant me serenity to accept the things I cannot change, courage to change the things I can, and wisdom to know the difference."

Praying this prayer should help us quickly overcome the pain someone has inflicted upon us, even though it's not as simple as it sounds. Let me help: it's easier than we think. I'm going to break this prayer down to hopefully spark a deeper understanding of how it can help us heal.

Many people follow world trends without completely understanding the trends they follow or why they're conforming to the ways of the world. The same goes for this prayer. It's often recited — sometimes daily, but do we understand what we're praying?

God, grant me the serenity. What does serenity mean? It's the state of calmness, peace, and being untroubled. Serenity is crucial, even in the midst of chaos. Even when we're being lied to and broken, maintaining serenity is paramount. Trust me; it took cultivating a personal relationship with God for me to learn what serenity is. I won't lie; it can be daunting. We'll fail many times before truly achieving it, but it is attainable.

Serenity helps control our emotions after discovering a lie. We tend to want to confront the person who lied to us, asking why they hurt us. That only sets us up to be lied to by the same person because most liars don't change, unless they find Jesus.

The next part of this prayer is **accepting the things I cannot change**. Accepting the things we can't change means: **not trying to change somebody**.

I'm very guilty of trying to change people. Instead of accepting them for who they are, I attempt to mold them into who I want them to be so I can continue to love them. Lack of acceptance is another way we set ourselves up for disappointment. Once we catch a liar in the inaugural untruth, we can almost bet there will be plenty more lies to follow.

Either accept them for who they are or let them go.

Cutting the cord can save years of heartache and pain if we just do it.

Don't worry. God will replace them with a better person.

A God-ordained mate.

The only one we have the power to change is ourselves. If we're unhappy with our life, change it. If we don't like who we are, change it. If we don't like our job, change it.

We have control over all of these circumstances and situations. If we let them ride as is, we're setting ourselves up for disappointment. This is where the third part of the prayer is derived from: **Courage to change the things I can**.

It takes courage to be ourselves and not conform:

"Do not conform to the pattern of this world, but be transformed by the renewing of your mind. Then you will be able to test and approve what God's will is—His good, pleasing, and perfect will."

Romans 12:2

For many years, I shied away from being who God said I was. I was the person people told me to be rather than who God created me to be. I ended up lost and confused for over thirty-five years, trying to figure out who I was. I searched the world, but the one person who held the answers I sought was God. The One who created me. When figuring out who we are, the best place to begin is with God. He designed us and knew who we were before we knew ourselves.

Remember, we only have control over and can change ourselves. Most of us have difficulty doing that. However, we can avoid years of trauma by focusing on ourselves instead of other people. Listen, we can't prevent people from lying to us. It's inevitable. We just have to learn to accept people for who they are and decide whether to leave or stay with them. Keep in mind whatever decision we make affects our lives, whether positive or negative. Don't blame the other person for what we've allowed.

This brings me to the final part of the prayer: **Wisdom to know the difference.** If you haven't asked God for wisdom, do it NOW. It's crucial. What is wisdom? Experience, knowledge, and good judgment — the quality of being wise.

Wisdom defines character. Some of us have wisdom way beyond our years, and then there are those who lack it. The wise should consider themselves blessed. It's a gift many don't have. Wisdom helps spot a lie. If we're wise, we don't have to worry about a liar clinging to us very long. Keep calling out their untruths, and eventually, they'll remove themselves from our life. Liars don't like wise people because they're not easily manipulated, and it makes them angry.

Praying for wisdom changes our perspective, our perception of people, and our worldly view.

CHAPTER EIGHT

Journal Talk with God After the Chaos

Dear God,

It's been a while since we talked. I've been spending time reading Your word, but I don't feel Your presence. It's been two years since I filed for divorce, and my marriage ended. I'm not sure if that was the right thing to do. Where are You, God? Do You hear me? My life's getting better; things are going back to normal. My children and I have our own home again. Hello, God. Are You there?

God, how did You expect me to stay married to a man who I caught with two different women? I begged You to reveal the things he was doing, and You showed me everything. Then why do I still feel so guilty about getting divorced? Was I wrong? Why do I feel this way?

Are You angry with me? I don't feel Your presence and can't hear You speaking. I'm sorry, God! What was I supposed to do? He threw me away like I was trash. What should I have done differently? I've been praying for direction and believe I'm going in the direction You want me to go. You told me to be still and know that You are God. (Psalms 46:10)

Please, Lord, don't be mad at me. I apologize for disappointing You. I honestly didn't mean to get divorced. I fought for my marriage, but how was I supposed to fight for it alone? I took my vows seriously and meant every word I said.

I have so many questions as to why Kevin did me this way. I know I'm not the only divorced woman in the world. I'm not asking for sympathy, but I'm angry, sad, tired, and weak. This isn't what I imagined my life being. Divorced. Why did this happen? Why do people hurt other people? God, this can't be the plan You designed for my life. God answers:

"For I know the plans I have for you," declares the Lord, "plans to prosper you and not harm you, plans to give you hope and a future."

Jeremiah 29:11

It was at this moment that I realized I needed to stop questioning God. Divorce was never His plan for my life. God wasn't mad at me.

God hates divorce, not the divorcee.

BETRAYAL

I trusted Kevin. I trusted my friends. I trusted my family.

...I trusted everyone.

I've trusted every single person in my life, and I'm loyal to a fault. Loyalty comes naturally to me. I'm the woman with a big heart, and I refuse to change the way I love others simply because I continue getting hurt by folk who don't know how to love or be loved.

Why are people so evil? Having a huge heart can poison discernment. How does it feel to be on the receiving end of betrayal? It made me feel like I'm the one who did something wrong. I was angry, sad, bitter, and sometimes ready to kill. Of course, I'm not going to kill anybody, but I do get angrier with myself than at the person who betrayed me. I'll forgive the person who did me wrong before forgiving myself.

It doesn't make sense, does it? I know! It doesn't make sense to me, either. I never understood why it's so hard for me to forgive myself, yet forgive the person who wronged me, even considering befriending them again — with limitations in place, of course. Once you've lost my trust, I'll never trust you again, but the Bible says not to hold a grudge against anyone.

"Let all bitterness and wrath and anger and clamor and slander be put away from you, along with all malice. Be kind to one another, tenderhearted, forgiving one another, as God in Christ forgave you."

Ephesians 4:31-32

As powerful as those words are, actually following the direction is an entirely different thing. However, it's something we all need to learn to do so we don't miss out on our blessings. I don't know about you, but I need all of mine.

When Kevin and I first met, I considered him to be honest. He'd never do anything to hurt me…that's the amount of trust I had in him. He seemed so sincere. Later, I discovered this was his lifestyle. Pursuing various women, plotting to get what he wants out of them. Once he gets what he wants, he leaves them empty. You've got to be a special kind of evil to prey on a person's heart.

Men aren't the only ones who are deceptive. Women do the same things. Emotionally unavailable, abusive, finding men they can use. In spite of it all, I refuse to give up on love.

I've experienced broken heart after broken heart, but I still believe in love. There are good men and women in this world. God willing, I'll get married again someday. I won't let a few bad relationships harden my heart. I'll never stop loving people, no matter how bad they treat me. God is love, and He lives within me. So, I'll continue displaying His love to bring light into this evil world. I've learned to let God take care of people who treat me bad and betray me, because His Word says so.

"Repay no one evil for evil but give thought to do what is honorable in the sight of all. If possible, so far as it depends on you, live peaceably with all. Beloved, never avenge yourselves, but leave it to the wrath of God, for it is written, 'Vengeance is mine, I will repay, says the Lord.' To the contrary, "if your enemy is hungry, feed him; if he is thirsty, give him something to drink; for by so doing you will heap burning coals on his head." Do not be overcome by evil, but overcome evil with good."

Romans 12:17-21

I can honestly say I've lived by these scriptures, even when it wasn't easy. I don't have enough fingers or toes to count how many times who has betrayed me, but I can tell you how many times I've wanted to do them just as bad or worse than they did me. I ultimately let God handle it His way, and He did far more than I could've done myself.

Betrayal hurts like H.E.L.L. It's the worst feeling in the world, especially when it comes from someone who says they love you. The term *I love you* is used so loosely today. If we don't mean it, we shouldn't say it because it can either uplift a person or destroy them. Can we honestly say we know the meaning of those words? If currently in a relationship or married, are we being loved correctly? I certainly hope so. Heartbreak is the worst pain to overcome. It doesn't matter the source; betrayal is betrayal, and it hurts!

I'll be the first to admit I don't know what love is. I don't know how it truly feels to be loved correctly. I do know how to love — much of it birthed through pain, but I've learned.

I learned how to display love because I never want anyone to experience the level of hurt and pain I've experienced from people claiming to love me.

Have you ever given someone your all and ended up with nothing left? That was me when I gave Kevin (who claimed to love me) everything I had to offer, only to end up mentally, physically, financially, and emotionally bankrupt, with absolutely nothing left for myself. We can't ever love someone else more than we love ourselves. Love yourself more. I'm not saying be selfish; I'm saying God didn't create us to be used, abused, and mistreated. He endured those things for us and created us to love and be loved. If we're being mistreated, it's okay to leave the situation. *We deserve better.*

"Beloved, let us love one another, for love is from God, and whoever loves has been born of God and knows God."

1 John 4:7

Remember this scripture the next time someone says *I love you.* Think about it: are they displaying God's love? If not, it may be rooted in the devil. Remember, the devil manifests as whatever we desire.

"The devil comes only to steal and kill and destroy."
John 10:10

Marriage helped me understand this scripture. Before saying "*I do*," I was single, happy, and enjoying life. A few years ago, a wise woman told me to be careful who we allow into our lives and who we let in our house.

What she meant didn't make sense to me until I hit rock bottom and ended up the same angry, unhappy, sad, miserable person I once was. Not because of things I'd done to myself, but because of what was done to me. I found myself healing from the same pain I had been delivered from. I'm not blaming anyone for what happened to me; my intent is to make it clear that depending on people can disrupt your happiness. We can be the most confident person in the world, but inviting in the wrong people can knock us down to unrecoverable levels.

Being bankrupt from betrayal is hard to overcome. It takes strength, determination, and hard work. Betrayal breeds depression; some days are better than others. Many of us blame ourselves for being betrayed. The truth is, betrayal has nothing to do with us. No matter how good we are to people, the possibility of them betraying us remains. Often, we're not even the only victim of their deception.

For some people, betrayal is a lifestyle. We shouldn't blame ourselves. Remember, we can't control how folk treat us. However, we can learn from it and keep it from happening again.

Overcoming betrayal affects us mentally. Altering the way we think after we are hurt requires a measure of strength we have to prepare for, especially to keep from blaming ourselves. No matter what the circumstance is, it's not our fault. We are NOT to blame and did nothing wrong. It's okay to kick, cry, and scream after being betrayed. Just don't stay there. The longer we blame ourselves, the more we'll entertain depression. Remember: therapy is normal. Investing in our healing through counseling helps move our lives forward.

It took an entire year for me to journey back towards myself. I had to learn how to accept an apology I was never going to receive. I had to go through the healing process again. Old wounds I thought I had healed from reopened, and I had to learn how to deal with them once more. I hit rock bottom again. Every time I have hit rock bottom, it was from my bad decisions and whom I placed my trust in.

Like Kevin.

Shockingly, I don't believe my marriage was a bad decision. When Kevin slid the ring on my finger, I thought it would be forever. Like most people do in relationships, I became comfortable, thinking marriage changes the rules of love. We need to understand that whatever we do to make a person fall in love with us has to be consistently present throughout the relationship.

Our feelings change daily, which explains how couples fall in and out of love. Falling in love is the easy part; staying in love when your mate isn't being loving is what's hard. That's where many marriages and relationships fall apart. I knew my marriage ending wasn't my fault, and I hadn't done anything wrong. I love with everything in me, but sometimes love isn't enough. Some people will continue to search the world for something deeper, only to end up with nothing.

My marriage wasn't the only place where I experienced betrayal. I got hit by friends and family, too. Never get too comfortable after healing. I thought I was healed, that is until the next time I was betrayed. It was harder to get over this time because of the vows attached to it, but I did it with hope, determination, God's strength, and standing on His word.

This time, I was able to heal for good. If I'm ever betrayed again (prayerfully not), I'll handle it way differently. For one thing, now I realize the way a person treats me is more telling of their character than mine. Now I know not to take betrayal personally because it's not my fault. I may not be able to stop someone from mistreating me, but what I can do is control my response, which means commanding my emotions. As a result, I'm more cautious of the people I surround myself with and pay better attention to the red flags and warning signs, because we all come with them.

CHAPTER NINE

Journal Talk with God After the Chaos

Dear God,

It's been five months since my divorce was final and two years since my marriage ended. Who knew I would come out of the betrayal, abandonment, and financial crises better than I was before? Losing everything except my mind (and some days I felt like I was losing it), I had to start life all over again completely. Now I understand the importance of new beginnings. It has allowed me to build myself up better. I understand my value as a person now because material things come and go.

God, I still don't understand why my divorce happened, but now I get the importance of being equally yoked. What do I do with my life now, God? Where do I go from here? I've lost everyone but You, God. I need Your help! I've lost my purpose. Why am I here? What am I supposed to be doing now that I'm single again? Do you hear me, God? I realize that people will come in and out of my life, and I have to learn to be okay with it. But, God, I need Your help to know who is seasonal and who's with me for a lifetime.

I strive daily not to put anything or anyone before You, God. I can't do that to You because when everyone left me, You were right here. As I continue reading Your word daily, I keep Your promises near and dear to my heart. You told me in Deuteronomy 31:8 that You go before me and will always be with me. You said You will not leave or forsake me, and for me not to fear or be dismayed.

God, I'll never forget the trouble, being lost, the taste of ashes, and the poison I've swallowed. I remember it all. Oh, how well I remember the feeling of hitting the bottom. But there's one thing I remember that helps me keep a grip on hope. (Lamentations 3:21-23)

How do I start over after a divorce? Don't You think I've suffered enough, God?

God finally speaks:

"My child, now that you have suffered a little while, the God of all grace, who has called you to His eternal glory in Christ, will Himself restore, confirm, strengthen, and establish you." (1 Peter 5:10)

"For I consider that the sufferings of this present time are not worth comparing with the glory that is to be revealed to us." (Romans 8:18)

"And we know that for those who love God all things work together for good, for those who are called according to His purpose." (Romans 8:28)

I knew everything was going to be alright, and things were going to get better. How was I so sure? Because God does His best work when we're weak, and Lord knows I was the weakest I'd ever been.

The reason God favors us in our weakness is because when we are full of ourselves, we act as though we don't need Him. Being full of pride and boastfulness as if we've got ourselves completely together isn't His will for us. Then when our lives fall apart or when trials flip our worlds upside down, we call on the Lord as an afterthought.

If it weren't for my relationship with God, I honestly wouldn't know He was working everything out for my good.

"He gives strength to the weary and increases the power of the weak."

Isaiah 40:29

"My flesh and my heart may fail, but God is the strength of my heart and my portion forever."

Psalm 73:26

"Come to Me, all you who are weary and burdened, and I will give you rest."

Matthew 11:28

"Cast all your anxiety on Him because He cares for you."

1 Peter 5:7

Daily scripture reading gave me hope. Yes, I was suffering, but the more I believed God's Word, the more my life started changing.

"Not only so, but we also glory in our suffering, because we know that suffering produces perseverance; perseverance, character; and

character, hope. And hope does not put us to shame,
because God's love has been poured out into our
hearts through the Holy Spirit, who has been given
to us."

Romans 5:3-5

This scripture taught me I had no reason to be ashamed of what had happened to me, and I wasn't. The people who knew my story would ask me how I was doing as if they were waiting for me to fall apart, giving me the motivation to succeed even more. I remember people saying, "Well, you look good." It was as if they wanted me to appear beat down and depressed — almost as if my suffering should be on display so they could see it. Their intrusion gave me even more motivation to make it.

THE DIVORCE

Prior to marrying Kevin, I tried handling our relationship in a Godly fashion. No sex before marriage; no living together. We even attended church together every Sunday. There was no way I knew I was dating the devil until time showed me.

After we married, Kevin and I moved in together at the house I had rented for six years. It was a nice size for us until we found a different home. Kevin handled our finances, and I was in complete agreement with it. Our marriage was going well. We enjoyed lots of family vacations, and his daughter spent weekends with us. Life was great!

…until it wasn't.

One day, I received a call from a woman asking if Kevin was available to talk. I explained she had called his wife's phone, and that's when the fun began.

Once I mentioned that I was his wife, the woman's agitation barreled through the line. When I asked her what she needed, she explained that she was Kevin's ex-wife and the mother of his three children who lived in St. Louis, Missouri. She went on about how she had been trying to contact Kevin to advise him that she was pregnant with his fourth child.

Imagine, if you will, getting a call from your husband's pregnant mistress. Kevin and I had only been married for a year; we were obviously newlyweds at the point of conception. Although I was mortified, I didn't yell, scream, or cuss the woman — most likely out of shock. Instead, I began asking her questions. The more questions I asked, the more she revealed about my husband.

The things this woman relayed to me about Kevin blew my mind. I didn't know what to believe. The only child he ever told me about was his daughter. Shoot, he never even mentioned he had been married before. I let his ex finish answering my questions and was polite as we spoke. She said what she had to say, and I disconnected the call.

Kevin was still at work when this went down. Not wanting to bother him with this drama while he was on the clock, I waited until he got home.

When he arrived, I greeted him the same as I did any other day. We discussed dinner, and he went to freshen up. While he was in the bathroom, he asked me how my day was.

"Great," I told him with a smile in my voice, "until a lady named Patricia called looking for you on my phone."

The toilet flushed, and then I heard the water running. Before I knew it, Kevin flung the bathroom door open so hard that it slammed into the wall. I thought he was going to pull it off its hinges, his face looking as if he had seen a ghost.

"Patricia?" he stuttered. "How did she get your phone number? Why did she call you? What did she say?" Kevin fired off question after question, not giving me a chance to respond to any of them.

"Kevin!" I shrieked, prompting him to freeze with his jaw dropped.

We stood in silence, staring at each other. I was speechless, not knowing where to begin sorting this mess out. I could tell Kevin was in shock, so I finally broke the silence.

"Clearly, you know that woman," I hissed, "There's got to be some truth to what she said."

"And what exactly did she say?" Kevin asked, his lips quivering as if he was on the verge of tears.

"That she's your ex-wife and pregnant with your fourth child," I spat. "Why did you lie to me about your life, Kevin? Who are you?"

The more questions I fired, the angrier Kevin got. Instead of confirming or denying my interrogation, Kevin hopped in his car and left. I never saw or heard from him again until the day we went to court to finalize the divorce.

Divorce and separation are hard situations to overcome. We grapple with whether to go or stay. We may be fighting for our marriage while our spouse is not. Emotions are swirling, and we can't regain control. Christians facing divorce worry about disappointing God and question if He'll be mad at us for divorcing.

Aside from disappointing God, I struggled with the fact that I thought I married the man God ordained for me. Too bad our entire union was based on lies.

Biblically, I had every reason to file for a divorce — namely, adultery.

Being equally yoked in a relationship is extremely important.

"Do not be unequally yoked with unbelievers. For what partnership has righteousness with lawlessness? Or what fellowship has light with darkness?"

2 Corinthians 6:14

I didn't think Kevin and I were unequally yoked until I discovered his lies. When dating, it's imperative to make sure our beliefs match. I'm not condemning believers for marrying non-believers, but God's word says:

"If any woman has a husband who is an unbeliever, and he consents to live with her, she should not divorce him. For the unbelieving husband is made holy because of his wife, and the unbelieving wife is made holy because of her husband."

1 Corinthians 7:13-14

It's not my place to advise anyone whom they should marry or what they should do with their life.

All I can do is share my testimony with you and pray you never have to experience the heartache I went through. There were days I prayed and asked God to please forgive me for filing for divorce. While sitting in my room at my father's house reading my Bible one day, God showed me why it was okay for me to file for divorce.

"But if the unbeliever leaves, let it be so. The brother or sister is not bound in such circumstances; God has called us to live in peace."

1 Corinthians 7:15

That was the day that I received the peace that surpasses all understanding. The scripture granted me peace, knowing I was a good wife. If you know you've been good to someone, whether it's a friend, husband, or wife, come to peace with the situation and move on when it's over. Sooner or later, that person will recognize what they've lost. If they don't, that's alright, too. Whatever you do, don't act out because someone treated you terribly. There are enough rude and evil people in the world. Be the kind light the world needs.

Just because my marriage ended in divorce doesn't mean yours will, too. If you're married and you genuinely love each other, fight for your marriage. It's better for two people to fight for their marriage than one. Marriage is a beautiful thing. I pray everyone who desires will be married one day, and I pray God sends a soulmate with who you are equally yoked.

CHAPTER TEN

Journal Talk with God After the Chaos

Dear God,

I'm dealing with the spirit of loneliness again. Even though it has been a few years since my marriage ended, I'm still dealing with residual pain. Lord, I'm asking for Your help in dealing with my abandonment and rejection issues. I often catch myself questioning why me, when I've been created in Your image to walk this earth for You. I get it, but why so much pain?

God, I know the Christian walk is a lonely one. I'm not asking to be surrounded by people; I just want to be loved, Lord. Is that asking too much? When will *someone come into my life and stay, God? When will I stop being used and abused? God, I hope You see that I'm trying to live my life right and according to the purpose and plans You have for me.*

God, I feel myself losing sight of what I am supposed to be doing. I'm weak, Lord! I don't want to slip into depression. God, help me to forgive him, and most importantly, please help me to forgive myself. God, I need You again, just like I did before. God, Your Word says to be kind to one another, tenderhearted, and forgiving as You forgave me. (Ephesians 4:32) I've done just those things. I've been kind, and yet, I still get treated like I'm nobody. God, help me, please! What do You want me to do?

God finally speaks:

"But I say to you who hears, love your enemies, do good to those who hate you."

Luke 6:27

"But I say to you, love your enemies and pray for those who persecute you."

Matthew 5:44

"Repay no one evil for evil, but give thought to do what is honorable in the sight of all."

Romans 12:17

After losing my home, I went to live with my father for nine months. I felt like a complete failure, but I still had hope! It turns out the facility where I stored our things was infested with bed bugs. I had nothing but my clothes and my car. I completely lost everything that I worked for years to establish. But through it all, God's unchanging word reminded me that I wasn't a failure.

I remember sitting in my room at my father's house, trying to make sense of everything that had happened. I know I made mistakes in my marriage — no one is perfect. I would lie on my bed for hours, listening to gospel music when I was all prayed out. I didn't know what else to pray for. I had already prayed the angry prayer, the crying prayer, the "why me" prayer, the sad prayer, the healing prayer, the forgiveness prayer, and the "what am I supposed to do" prayer. Every prayer you can think of, I prayed. Since God knows everything, He also knew I was tired of praying.

"In the same way, the Spirit helps us in our weakness. We do not know what we ought to pray for, but the Spirit himself intercedes for us through wordless groans."

Romans 8:26

God intercedes on our behalf even when we're too tired to pray.

When we reach the breaking point past prayer, consider what Romans 8:26-28 says: *"Meanwhile, the moment we get tired in the waiting, God's Spirit is right alongside helping us along."*

When we don't know how or what to pray, God prays for us through our groans. He knows us far better than we know ourselves. This is why we can be certain that He has worked everything out for our good. When I got tired of praying, I turned on my gospel music and praised God through singing.

God knew that one of my heart's desires was to have an intimate relationship with my father. While living with him, I was able to learn so much about myself. There were things that I never fully comprehended about myself until I lived with my father, which also showed me who he was and where I got some of my ways.

Living with my father was a blessing. We didn't discuss my marriage, but we did talk about God. It was he who helped increase my understanding of the Bible as we sat in his room studying on his bed. He introduced me to various scriptures and taught me so much.

When I woke up some mornings, I would catch

Dad kneeling on the side of his bed, praying. He taught me not to read the Bible but to study it. That's when God provided me with the wisdom to understand His words. And it came through my father.

God can and will use anyone.

FORGIVENESS

After the divorce was final, the healing process began. The first step was forgiveness, which comes naturally for me. I'm a very caring and understanding person when it comes to people, which is probably why I tend to get mistreated. I can't help it — it's who I am. Years ago, I learned forgiveness after surviving domestic violence. My real hurdle is learning to forgive myself for dealing with less than I deserve.

Forgiveness is paramount because it delivers our heart from hurt, anger, bitterness, and deceitfulness. Forgiveness is more for us than the other person. I have learned to accept apologies I may never receive. Without forgiveness, we block the blessings God has for us. God speaks to our hearts; we can't hear Him clearly through an unforgiving heart filled with anger and bitterness.

So many of us struggle with forgiveness. Our first instinct is to get someone back for doing us dirty.

How do I know? Because I've had revengeful thoughts, too. But the best revenge is to walk away and carry on with life. Leave vengeance to God.

"Beloved, never avenge yourselves, but leave it to the wrath of God, for it is written, 'Vengeance is mine; I will repay,' says the Lord."

Romans 12:19

This scripture is so true; I have seen it manifest many times. Society calls it karma, and it's real.

I had a hard time forgiving myself because I was wrapped up in trying to figure out where I went wrong. What could I have done differently to prevent it from happening? The truth of the matter is, it would've happened no matter what I did.

My marriage would have ended no matter what because it was pre-ordained that way. Although it was devastating, it was destiny. We get so caught up in trying to keep people in our lives who don't want to stay, but we can't make anyone love us. That's how we get stressed — trying to make folk treat us a certain way, and when they don't, we feel unwanted.

There are over a billion people in the world. Just because one person rejects us doesn't mean we're unlovable. Let that person go. I wasted time stressing myself out, trying to do everything to please people, and nothing I did was good enough. The greatest power is learning to love ourselves. Once we master that, it will make more sense to us when people leave our lives. When we truly love ourselves, we learn who we are, as well as our worth. Everyone isn't meant to be part of our lives forever.

We get seasonal people mixed up with lifetime people. Every person we encounter isn't meant to be there for a lifetime. This is one of my absolute biggest mistakes I make often. I love to love people. So many people in this world are hurting, and I'm that person who wants to fix every person in my life, which always leaves me drained.

Forgiveness doesn't happen overnight. It's like a full-time job meant to be worked daily. Forgiveness happens in steps. There is power in forgiveness. Once we learn to forgive others as well as ourselves, there's a release. Holding grudges may be much easier to do; however, forgiveness doesn't mean forgetting what was done to us or keeping our betrayers in our lives. It won't even change your feelings about the situation.

We're human. We're allowed to feel a certain way about the situation; we just can't let our feelings stop us from pushing past it. It's alright to cry, kick, or scream if we must; we simply can't stay there. And once we forgive someone, it doesn't mean staying in contact with them. Forgiveness is NOT for the person who hurt you. Forgiveness is about you and only for you. We'll never forget what happened, but forgiving frees us from bondage and bitterness.

Now to get my life back in order, I had to exercise forgiveness. I knew God wasn't going to bless me or turn my life around if my heart was filled with resentment and anger. How could I ask Him to forgive me without forgiveness in my own heart? Where would I be today if God hadn't forgiven me for all the wrong I've done? I'm not perfect, but I've asked forgiveness for the pain I've caused people, too. Thank God there's no limit to forgiveness, or we would all probably be dead.

I hear people say all the time, "They don't deserve my forgiveness!" or "Why should I forgive them?" I used to say those things, too, until becoming a child of God. I had no intentions of forgiving those who hurt me. I have experienced way more pain in my life than pleasure; however, I've forgiven everyone who has hurt me. If I hadn't, I would still be unhappy, angry, and bitter while they went on with their lives. I have even asked God why I must forgive, and He told me:

"In prayer there is a connection between what God does and what you do. You cannot get forgiveness from God, for instance, without also forgiving others. If you refuse to do your part, you cut yourself off from God's part."

Matthew 6:14-15

We have all heard that we're not supposed to question God. Well, I do. How can we lean unto His understanding if we don't ask to find out what it is? We may not get an immediate response, and it may not be the answer we're in search of — if we even get one. No matter the outcome, we are allowed to ask God questions; I question Him all the time.

Sometimes, we refuse to forgive the person who has wronged us because it's a sense of security and safety — a way to let the other person know they don't have the power to hurt us any longer. In the end, holding onto that power hurts us more than it hurts the other person. Let it go.

"Let all bitterness and wrath and anger and clamor and slander be put away from you, along with all malice. Be kind to one another, tenderhearted, forgiving one another, as God in Christ forgave you."

Ephesians 4:31-32

109

As God's Word tells us, forgiveness doesn't cancel boundaries. For instance, for me not to get drawn into the painful memories of how things used to be, could have been, or how I wanted them to be, I had to separate my emotions from reality. Often, we justify unforgiveness based on how we've been mistreated. We can put boundaries in place, but we must forgive.

My boundaries were blocking my ex from bouncing in and out of my life. Unless a person changes after they've been forgiven, we have to stop them from dropping in and out of our lives when it's convenient for them. This only keeps the wounds open, which could be healed if the person would stay away. Without boundaries, we're held in bondage, inviting bitterness, resentment, anger, and revenge to flood our hearts, ending in unforgiveness. Unforgiveness holds us hostage if we allow it.

Why is it so hard to forgive?

Pride plays a big part in our hesitance to forgive others. Years and months after the offense can fly by, and we still hold grudges because of our pride. Pride is the reason many marriages, friendships, and other relationships fail, even after forgiving.

What is pride?

There are two ways to define pride.

Pride is deep pleasure or satisfaction derived from one's achievements, the achievements of those with whom one is closely associated, or from qualities or possessions that are widely admired. Pride is also having confidence and self-respect as expressed by members of a group — typically one that has been socially marginalized — based on their shared identity, culture, and experience. Pride is preferring self-will instead of the will of others or the Will of God.

The reason pride affects our relationships is that it makes people feel superior to others or provokes them to think others are less intelligent than them. Pride also breeds out-of-control egos and will have us saying, "I'm not the problem; they are."

None of us is perfect. Every one of us has wronged somebody, and it's much easier for us to blame the other person we're at odds with than to admit our own mistakes or that we were wrong.

Pride is deceptive. It prevents us from spotting our wrongs and considering the other person's feelings or viewpoint. Forgiveness requires humility and meekness; we all need to recognize our imperfections — flaws and all. I'm certain my past relationships (friend, family, ex-husband, or otherwise) may feel like I did something wrong to make them leave my life. No matter what the reason was behind the relationship ending, I've forgiven myself and them. I'm healed, and I'm free.

FORGIVENESS IS FOR YOURSELF!

CHAPTER ELEVEN

Journal Talk with God After the Chaos

Dear God,

I'm ready now.

I'm ready to begin my new life. I've forgiven him, but most importantly, I have forgiven myself. While not completely healed, I am healing and feel amazing. I'm not trying to get back to my old self because that part of me is gone. Lord, please make me new again. I want to thank You, God, for our new home. Thank You for sticking by my side when everyone else left me. I isolated myself as I went through the healing process because I didn't want to hurt others with my actions or words. I didn't want to hurt someone because I was in pain, so I understand why You separated me from everyone. I've lost so much these past few years, and as bad as it hurts, I consider it all a blessing now. I'll admit that losing everything ripped me apart, but I thank You, Lord, for taking it all away. All those material things I lost were attached to something or someone from my past that I needed to let go of. Now, everything in my home is brand new, with no strings or memories attached to them. I'm filled with so much joy, God, because starting over is truly bliss. I'm using the pain I've endured to fulfill my life's purpose.

As for the people who were once in my life whom I cared more about than they for me, I pray blessings and prosperity over their lives. If I caused them pain, God, I'm asking for Your forgiveness. Who knew being stripped of everything would bring me so many blessings and joy? I completely understand what letting go and letting God means now.

For three years, I've surrendered my life to You, the hardest thing I've ever done. I had no control — only faith. What looked like disaster and devastation ended up being my biggest blessing. Everything I endured prepared me for what came and is to come. God, I don't know where I'd be if I didn't have You. I'm absolutely nothing without You.

I'm ready for love now.

For over forty years, I've been learning how to be loved. How does it feel to be loved? I've figured it out. I know what love looks like now. Love is YOU. Now, in order to see love, I look for YOU. You love people with Your actions, and that's what I look for now. Once someone loves me with their actions, I see the love they have for me. God, You are amazing. Thank You so much for loving me.

LETTING GO!

Life is a roller coaster. Some people enjoy the ride with their hands up, laughing, and having a good time no matter what happens. Others struggle once they get off and never want to get on the ride again from fear of what they experienced the first time. I refuse to allow divorce or a bad marriage to stop me from loving again.

I want to get married again, and I will.

Divorce is a horrible thing for anyone to go through, but it's also rarely discussed. Divorce triggers emotional, mental, and financial effects that can be both draining and depressing. After my divorce, life seemed empty. I honestly didn't know where to start rebuilding my life. Although I was successful, I couldn't help feeling defeated.

While embarking upon video- and photoshoots, book tours, live interviews, and traveling to different states, I couldn't embrace my blessings. My whole life had fallen apart.

My emotions were all over the place; I felt like I would have a nervous breakdown, especially when I was forced to file for bankruptcy to get my life back on track.

It's imperative to control our emotions so that we won't react to the first punch when life knocks us down. Controlling our emotions gives us self-control. Reacting to every bad situation in life is a destructive path we don't need to take. Every event doesn't deserve a reaction; we must think first before responding.

I waited two years before filing for divorce, which was triggered by a woman calling my phone to advise she'd been in my house, in my bed with my ex-husband. The day after that phone call, I printed off the divorce papers online, drove to the courthouse, and paid the divorce fees. In sixty days, my divorce was final.

The dissolution of my marriage took sixty days to be finalized because when a spouse refuses to sign divorce papers, in some states, a "no-fault" divorce is declared, which means wrongdoing by either party doesn't have to be proven. The spouse requesting the divorce must tell the court that the marriage is irretrievably broken in order for it to go through. Because of this law, even if the opposing spouse refuses to sign the papers, the divorce will be final after sixty days.

Some may question why I waited so long to file for the divorce. It's simple; I never wanted it. I dreamt of a marriage that would last a lifetime. What if I had run with my emotions and filed for divorce as soon as we separated, then we agreed to work on our marriage months later? That would have meant getting remarried. Ultimately, infidelity on more than one occasion and adultery were my reasons for filing, even if it took a while. I understand the importance of patience and how it's a blessing to wait on God.

"Be still before the Lord and wait patiently for Him; fret not yourself over the one who prospers in His way, over the man who carries out evil devices! Refrain from anger and forsake wrath! Fret not yourself; it tends only to evil. For the evildoers shall be cut off, but those who wait for the Lord shall inherit land."

Psalms 37:7-9

I'm glad I waited as long as I did to file for divorce. Time reveals everything we need to know, as well as our level of patience. When I tell you that God revealed everything to me about my marriage while I waited, not once did I ever have to go and search, find, or look for anything. God revealed all of it to me. That's when I finally filed without guilt.

After the divorce was final, I set out to rebuild my life, starting with cleaning up the mess I created by filing for bankruptcy, which was finalized five months before my divorce. I thank God I waited on Him, or I don't believe my life would be where it is today. When I say my life is good, I'm not speaking materialistically. I'm referring to my newfound strength, my stronger relationship with Christ, the strengthened bond with my children, and my restored relationship with my father.

"But they who wait for the Lord shall renew their strength; they shall mount up with wings like eagles; they shall walk and not faint."

Isaiah 40:31

Now, my life has so much meaning. It's important to release what's hindering you, whether it's a person, place, or thing.

When I moved into my new place, I was sad because I had to get rid of all my old stuff. I questioned God yet again, asking Him why He allowed my belongings to be infested with bed bugs, resulting in me losing everything I worked so many years to build. He answered me, but it was not the answer I wanted.

God said, *"Do not lay up for yourselves treasures on earth, where moth and rust destroy and where thieves break in and steal, but lay up for yourselves treasures in heaven, where neither moth nor rust destroys and where thieves do not break in and steal. For where your treasure is, there your heart will be also."* *(Matthew 6:19-21)*

We live our lives building our treasures on earth, forgetting it is only temporary. When we die, we can't take anything with us but our souls. We forget that material possessions will always come and go, but the soul lasts forever.

"For what will it profit a man if he gains the whole world and forfeits his soul? Or what shall a man give in return for his soul?"

Matthew 16:26

After God spoke these words to me, my entire

perspective changed. What I lost was no longer important to me. God quickly replaced them with better things. When I moved into my new home, every room was fully furnished from front to back, with everything brand new.

God had supplied all of my needs.

When we let go and allow God to have His way in our lives, He gives us better than we had or imagined for ourselves. I had to be stripped of my possession in order to restart my life and focus on God. Those belongings came with bad memories attached to them. I was hanging onto things that old friends and boyfriends had given me, and for some reason, I was afraid to get rid of them, or I believed they had sentimental value. The truth is, I needed to get rid of it all to move forward.

How can we get a fresh start carrying around old possessions? I had to realize I wasn't just harboring old memories; I was dragging around old spirits from one place to another. I could never forget the past because I kept holding the past in my face. Do you have old possessions from an ex or former friend? Are you holding onto the past because you once had a good time with them?

Let it go!

"At all times, we must learn to forget the past and forge ahead. If we fail to let go of the past, it is exceedingly difficult to move forward."
                                    Isaiah 43:18-19

During my marriage, after I published my first book, and during my divorce, I lost many people I thought were my friends and cared about me — the very people I believed were going to be in my life forever. I told you that I lost everything. But I was more than ready for my new beginning. I was scared, but I leaned on my favorite scripture to help me through:

"Have I not commanded you? Be strong and courageous. Do not be frightened, and do not be dismayed, for the Lord your God is with you wherever you go."
                                    Joshua 1:9

I recite that verse a lot, knowing that the spirit of fear is not of God.

"God hath not given us the spirit of fear, but of power, and of love, and of a sound mind."
                                    2 Timothy 1:7

I didn't have a reason to fear. Of course, I didn't know where my life was headed, but I wasn't stressed because I trusted God. I had to; I didn't have the strength to handle anything on my own. The burden was too heavy for me; I had to give it all to Him.

I encourage anyone struggling with letting go of people, places, and things to ask God for guidance. Whatever disrupts our peace is not of God and needs to be removed from our lives. If it causes strife and chaos, diminishes our worth or who we are, it has got to go. If we have to question where we stand with someone, we should be direct and ask if they love us. If it comes down to telling them, "Please don't tell me you love me," because their actions don't make us feel loved, let them go. It's better to have peace than tolerate chaos.

"I have said these things to you, that in me you may have peace. In the world you will have tribulations. But take heart! I have overcome the world."

John 16:33

We can overcome the very thing we think we can't live without. We often pray to God to change someone or remove the person who's hurting us, but instead of letting them go when He removes them, we

122

hold on even tighter and then get angry because that person keeps hurting us. In the end, we blame God for not answering our prayers.

God answers every prayer we have — some quicker than others and not always in the way we expect. No matter when (or how) He answers, remember God loves us and wants the best for us. If He's telling you to let something go, DO IT. Get to your blessings.

There's power in letting go!

CHAPTER TWELVE

HOW I LEARNED PERSEVERANCE & BECAME RESILIENT

Once my life was back on track, I had so much joy. However, I can't say life was back to normal because it wasn't. In fact, life was totally different.

Although everything was now unfamiliar, I was still filled with joy and peace that surpasses all understanding.

"And the peace of God, which passes all understanding, shall keep your hearts and minds through Christ Jesus."

Philippians 4:7

Thank God for giving me peace in a storm. Without Him, I would've lost my mind and wouldn't be able to tell the story of how I became resilient and was able to persevere despite everything I battled. As bad as the situation was, I still came out on top and more blessed than before.

Through the fire, I've learned what perseverance and resilience means. I've worn the conqueror's crown my entire life. From this day forward, no matter what happens to me, I know how to persevere in any situation I face. What is perseverance? Perseverance is persistence despite difficulty or delay and coming out of it successfully.

How do we persevere?

The first step towards perseverance is never to give up or quit. Even when we're feeling defeated, and the situation doesn't seem as if it's ever going to improve, keep going. It will get better. It may not be overnight, in a week, in a month, or even in a year. But if we keep going, every step we take is a step closer towards a better life and breakthrough. Many people stop when they don't see immediate results; we can't do that to ourselves. Sooner than later, the results will manifest.

I could've given up, but why quit? That's the easy

way out.

Perseverance requires setting goals.

It doesn't matter how long or short term the goal is when we believe we will achieve it. Setting the goal is a step closer to completion. We can't allow how much work has to be put into the goals to deter us; that's where we get too stressed out to see the vision through. Eyeing the finish line instead of where we start is a natural deterrent. Negative thoughts lead to giving up. Ignore what the situation looks like. Better days are coming; think on that.

We must set our own pace. Getting caught up in society's timing causes us to miss out on our blessings. For example, if a friend marries in her thirties, we suddenly are in a rush to get to the altar with our groom or bride. Or maybe someone starts their business, and it turns out to be successful. Now we want to do the same. Suddenly, we're so caught up in what others have going on in their lives that ours ends up in shambles.

It took an entire year after my life fell apart before things changed for the better. Every home I looked at during the period when I was living with my father wasn't what I wanted or was out of my price range. Now I could've gone ahead of my goal just to get into my own place, but moving to a place I couldn't afford was only going to lead to more stress. Don't rush; timing is everything.

Don't worry about what the next person is doing or what they have to say about your situation. It's easy to say what we won't do or what we won't put up with in certain situations. The truth is, we never know how we'll react until we are faced with it. But stay focused and don't worry about the people who are laughing and talking. No matter how we live our lives, people will always have something to say about us. Just keep living.

The most important aspect of perseverance is living in the moment. Many of us live our lives in the past or worry so much about what will happen next that we don't enjoy life. Every day, life threw something at me, which caused things to get worse. I had no choice but to live in the moment, though, because each day was a burden that I had no control over.

"Therefore, do not worry about tomorrow, for tomorrow will worry about itself. Each day has enough trouble of its own."

Matthew 6:34

At one point, life got the best of me. My situation had gotten so bad that I stopped worrying about it. No matter what I did or how much I tried, life continued getting worse. Have you ever had a situation that, no matter how much you tried to change it for the better, it kept getting worse? When that happens, let go of the situation. Pray about it and give it to God; the problem is too big for you to handle. Stop stressing about it and live in the moment.

Living in the moment can be complicated. Some of us are diving so deep into our past that it disrupts focusing on today. Now some don't live in the past; however, they plan their lives so far ahead that when a single life change happens, or things don't go as planned, they quit — even though we're only supposed to live one day at a time.

"Do not be anxious about anything, but in everything by prayer and supplication, with thanksgiving, let your requests be made known to God."

Philippians 4:6

If we can persevere through challenges and setbacks, the better we become at it and as a person when problems arise. Perseverance requires self-control. Instead of lashing out and acting out of emotions, mastering perseverance allows us to analyze the situation before reacting. Whenever we experience adversity, we need to take a deep breath before reacting and ask ourselves if it is in our control.

We should concern ourselves with things in our control. If the problem is in our control, try to break down the problem.

Failure is a part of life, but always find a way to get back up. No matter how bad the situation may be, every problem has a solution. Sometimes, the solution is to let the problem go.

Heartbreak is probably one of the hardest things to persevere through. Love will break us down, but perseverance helps us become resilient. What is resilience? Resilience means being able to withstand or recover quickly from difficult conditions. It's someone or something that bounces back. Resilience gives us the strength to learn lessons from tough situations and move on when we fail.

Resilience allows us to reclaim our power to overcome setbacks. We'll experience numerous setbacks while learning this process. Listen, the children of Israel were in the wilderness for forty years. I endured forty years of setbacks before I became resilient. Heartbreak after heartbreak. Failure after failure. After each setback, I became stronger, wiser, and bounced back quicker each time.

Resilience requires being aware of ourselves. It's easier to point the blame at others for the wrong they've done to us, but self-awareness is necessary to become resilient. We need to become aware of our feelings, desires, urges, patterns, and thought process in order to gain complete control of our emotions.

Next, we need to refocus our attention. So much of our life is wasted focusing on things and people that don't hold any value to us. Then we wonder why we remain stuck where we are in life. I know it's much easier to create excuses than redirect our attention to the things that matter. But if we train ourselves to accept bad habits and bad people, we can develop and train ourselves to focus on what's now instead of focusing on the past, which leads to unhappiness and stress.

LET IT GO.

This brings me to my third point: letting go.

I know I discussed letting go in chapter eleven, but there are two ways to let go: physically or mentally. Most of us remove people, places, and things out of our lives physically but not mentally. Most of us have mastered physically letting someone go; it's the mental part of it that's a hurdle because of the emotions attached to it.

Some of us believe we've overcome someone or something, but something can arise to let us know that we haven't. I call these triggers. Triggers are negative or unhelpful beliefs that come back into our lives and cause us to lose focus. That's why it's important to deal with issues that affect us mentally. Even though I've gotten my life back on track physically, I still have some mental and emotional healing I must deal with. If something happens in my life similar to my divorce, I won't react out of my emotions and know how to handle the situation.

It took years before I realized my resilience. Not because I physically bounced back from all the bad situations, but because I internalized them. I've learned I have the ability to cope with tragedy and still achieve my goals. A resilient person may come off as a cocky or overconfident individual to society, which doesn't reflect true resilience. It's quite the opposite because resilient people know themselves and the potential they have. They don't wait for someone to tell them.

I can't be more thankful to God for giving me the strength and capability to learn how to heal. Love is a beautiful thing — especially when two people come together who not only love each other but respect and trust each other. One day, I'll be married again. I know people probably think I must be out of my mind, continuing to love after all I've endured. The truth is, each person showed me what love really is. Love isn't them. Love is me. I am love. My integrity, character, faith, strength in God, and kind soul — all those things in me is love. God told me: "Greater is He that is in me than He that is in the world." (1 John 4:4)

GOD IS LOVE.

"If I give everything I own to the poor and even go to the stake to be burned as a martyr, but I do not love, I have gotten nowhere. So, no matter what I say, what I believe, and what I do, I am bankrupt without love. Love never gives up. Love cares more for others than for self. Love does not want what it does not have. Love doesn't strut, doesn't have a swelled head, doesn't force itself on others, is not always "me first," doesn't fly off the handle, doesn't keep score of the sins of others, doesn't revel when others grovel, takes pleasure in the flowering of

truth, puts up with anything, trusts God always, always looks for the best, never looks back, but keeps going to the end."

1 Corinthians 13 3-7

So now faith, hope, and love abide, these three; but the greatest of these is love.

1 Corinthians 13:13

Beloved, let us love one another, for love is from God, and whoever loves has been born of God and knows God.

1 John 4:7

A new commandment I give to you, that you love one another: just as I have loved you, you also are to love one another.

1 John 13:34

Above all, keep loving one another earnestly, since love covers a multitude of sins.

1 Peter 4:8

Let all that you do be done in LOVE.

1 Corinthians 16:14

About the Author

Seant'a Conyers is a Woman of God, a loving mother of two boys, an award-winning author, an award-winning community leader, a CASA (Court Appointed Special Advocate) for abused and neglected children, a speaker, and the owner & operator of S.L.A.Y FASHIONS, her online boutique. Seant'a has volunteered over 2,000 hours of mentoring to help women and children in her community.

Seant'a is from a small town in Indiana called Kokomo. She is the author of her award-winning book titled *Being Pretty Is Hard Work, Broken Psalms 51:17,* and *Please! Don't Say You Love Me.* She began writing in 2015, after becoming an ugly woman on the inside from dealing with her own bad life experiences. Her books are non-fiction self-help books based on true stories about her life. After a one-year marriage that ended in divorce and caused Seant'a to become mentally, emotionally, and financially bankrupt, Seant'a found her purpose in life, which was birthed from her pain. Today, she is an overcomer of homelessness, divorce, and a survivor of domestic violence.

The purpose of Seant'a's books is to help others understand that true beauty and happiness come from within. She desires to help others overcome their hurts and pains. Seant'a reminds herself daily of her quote: "Being Pretty Is Not Worth the Work If You're Ugly on The Inside!" It helps her remain humble and reminds her that her scars are B.E.A.U.T.I.F.U.L. (Believer, Encourager, Anointed, Understanding, Trustworthy, Integrity, Favor, Unbroken, Loving) and her wounds have been healed with love.

Seant'a received her college education from Indiana Wesleyan University of Marion, Indiana, where she obtained her Associate of Science in

Business and a Bachelor of Science in Business Management. She later decided to continue her education and pursued her Master of Science in Public Affairs.

Seant'a began her mentoring organization in 2017 called Single Heart's Helping One, LLC. It is a developmental and mentoring program designed to help single women with children. Seant'a's vision for this program is to allow single women the opportunity to live their lives happy and prosperous with their children. It provides services and programs to help them become better parents, learn money management, obtain an education, achieve goals, and provide a better life for their children and themselves.

Seant'a's passion is to journey worldwide speaking, mentoring, motivating, and inspiring women of all ages, helping them pursue and accomplish their goals and dreams. Today, Seant'a is living and walking in the purpose that God has designed for her life. She is living life unbroken and filled with love.

Visit Seant'a's websites to learn more:
   https://seantaconyers.com
   www.slayfashions.com